S0-ANP-647

My First Words

to See and Learn

Illustrated by David Melling
Compiled by Neil Morris

PASSPORT BOOKS
NTC/Contemporary Publishing Group

For Bosiljka, Branko and Igor Sunajko.

D.M.

Library of Congress Cataloging-in-Publication Data

Morris, Neil, 1946–
    My first words to see and learn / illustrated by David Melling ;
compiled by Neil Morris. — US English ed.
      p.   cm.
    ISBN 0-8442-2405-7
    1. Vocabulary—Juvenile literature.   I. Melling, David.
II. Title.
PE1449.M635   1999
428.1—dc21   98-37176
                                          CIP

Printed in Italy

This US English Edition of *My First Book of Words* originally published in
English in 1999 is published by arrangement with Oxford University Press.

This edition published 1999 by Passport Books
A division of NTC/Contemporary Publishing Group, Inc.
4255 West Touhy Avenue, Lincolnwood (Chicago), Illinois 60646-1975 U.S.A.
Text copyright © 1999 by Neil Morris
Illustrations copyright © 1999 by David Melling

All rights reserved. No part of this book may be reproduced, stored in a
retrieval system, or transmitted in any form or by any means, electronic,
mechanical, photocopying, recording, or otherwise, without the prior
permission of NTC/Contemporary Publishing Group, Inc.

International Standard Book Number: 0-8442-2405-7

16   15   14   13   12   11   10   9   8   7   6   5   4   3   2   1

CENTRAL ARKANSAS LIBRARY SYSTEM
SHERWOOD BRANCH LIBRARY
SHERWOOD, ARKANSAS

Contents

Look at Me!

chest

leg

foot

toe

back

elbow

bottom

finger

tummy

knee

hand

hair

arm

head

shoulders

4

face

cheek

ear

eye

chin

mouth

teeth

tongue

neck

nose

girl

boy

Our House

roof

trash can

gate

stairs

chimney

fence

garage

window

door

dog

cat

rabbit

spider

snail

letters

mailbag

leaf

flower

tree

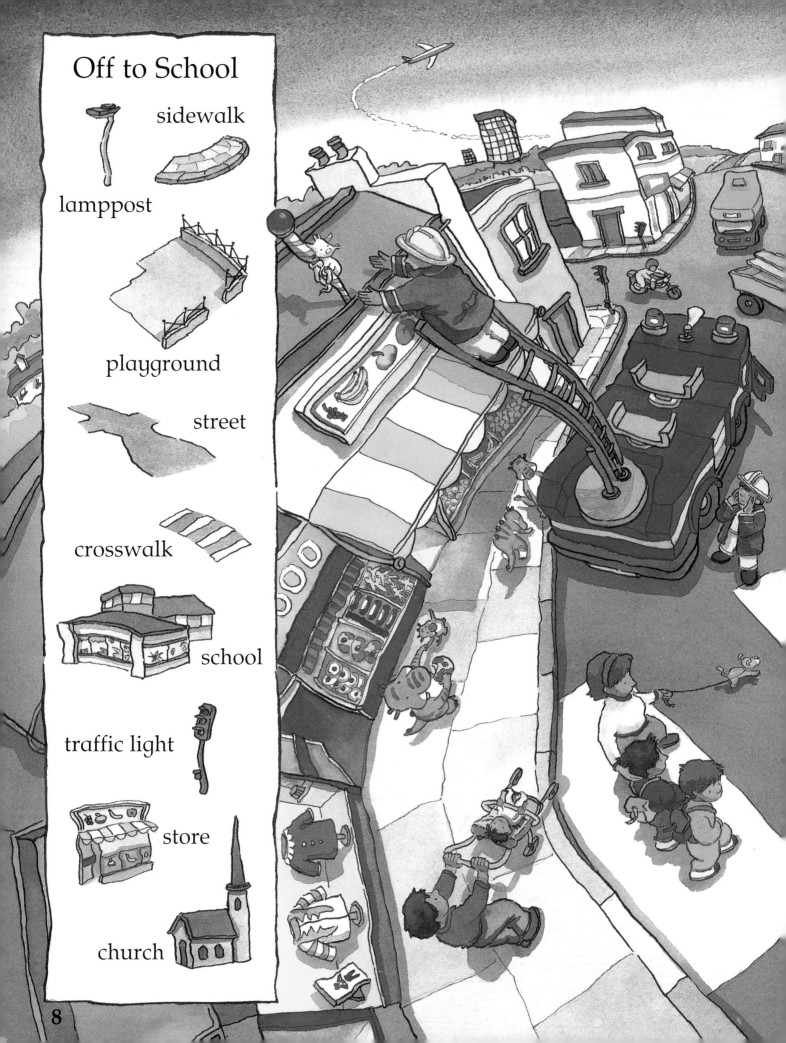

Off to School

sidewalk

lamppost

playground

street

crosswalk

school

traffic light

store

church

8

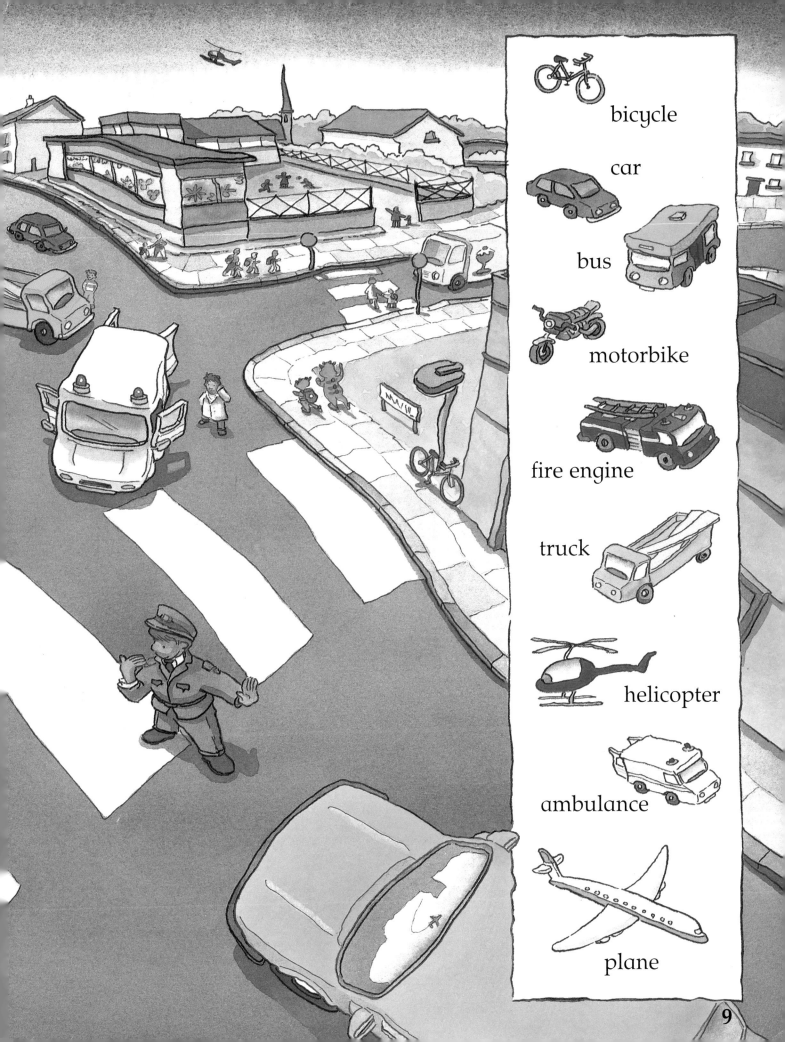

bicycle

car

bus

motorbike

fire engine

truck

helicopter

ambulance

plane

Our Classroom

backpack

book

lunch box

chalkboard

chalk

globe

desk

magnet

wastebasket

10

cassette player

cassette

ruler

computer

map

disk

dice

keyboard

mouse

11

Color Fun

black

blue

brown

green

gray

orange

pink

purple

red

white

yellow

12

smock

glue

painting

paintbrush

paints

pencil

paper

scissors

marker

easel

13

When I Grow Up

mailman

carpenter

doctor

police officer

vet

athlete

fire fighter

bus driver

14

engineer

pop star

pilot

dancer

diver

cook

astronaut

lifeguard

A Long Time Ago

Dinosaurs
200 million years ago

Tyrannosaurus Rex

Stegosaurus

Diplodocus

Triceratops skeleton

fossil

bone

The Stone Age
10,000 years ago

cave

flint

cave painting

fire

Ancient Egyptians
5,000 years ago

pyramid

sphinx

Pharoah

Ancient Romans
2,000 years ago

pottery

coins

soldier

Busy Shopping

shopping cart

basket

cash register

bread

bun

jam

cereal

potatoes

sausages

spaghetti

18

milk

yogurt

cheese

eggs

apple

banana

orange

tomato

carrot

lettuce

19

Monster Lunch

stove

refrigerator

washing machine

saucepan

iron

cup

bowl

knife

fork

kettle

plate

spoon

saucer

chair

teapot

cushion

sofa

stereo

table

television

VCR

vacuum cleaner

21

Time to Play

dollhouse

doll

game

race car

robot

jigsaw puzzle

teddy bear

train set

drum

guitar

keyboard

microphone

trumpet

recorder

cymbals

bells

tambourine

23

On the Farm

horse

chicken

rooster

duck

goose

sheep

goat

pig

cow

24

tractor

stream

bridge

field

forest

hay

hill

scarecrow

25

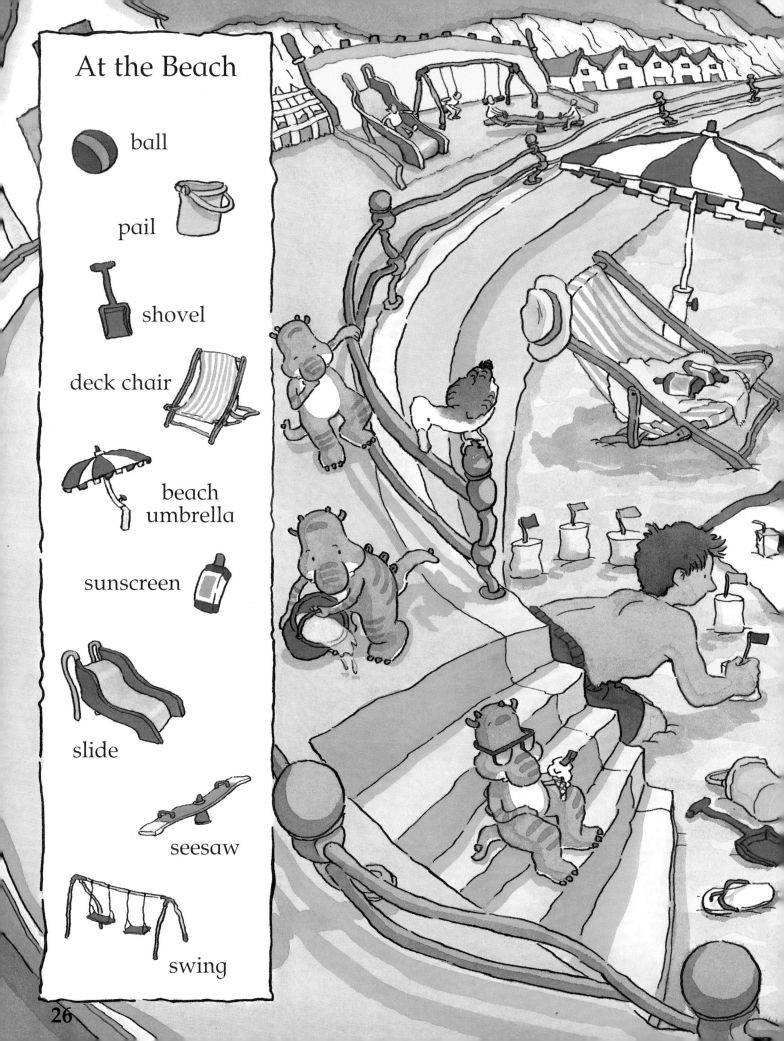

At the Beach

ball

pail

shovel

deck chair

beach umbrella

sunscreen

slide

seesaw

swing

ship

lighthouse

sandcastle

seagull

shell

crab

octopus

starfish

seaweed

Birthday Party

birthday card

candle

balloon

gift

streamer

noisemaker

party hat

wand

magician

28

candy

sandwich

pizza

ice cream

chocolate

cookie

straw

drink

cake

29

Animal Friends

elephant

crocodile

giraffe

fish

hippopotamus

kangaroo

monkey

koala bear

30

mouse

walrus

parrot

penguin

tiger

zebra

panda

rhinoceros

31

In the Bath

dress

jacket

sweater

shorts

underpants

shirt

shoes

skirt

socks

pants

T-shirt

sink

bathtub

washcloth

mirror

shower

soap

sponge

toilet

toilet paper

toothbrush

toothpaste

towel

Time for Bed

wardrobe

curtains

lamp

nightstand

pajamas

nightgown

pillow

bed

blanket

dresser

storybook

castle

king

queen

genie

magic lamp

dragon

giant

My ABCs

A a   ant

B b   bell

C c   caterpillar

D d   dog

E e   egg

F f   fish

G g   goat

H h   helicopter

I i   ink

J j   juggler

K k   king

L l   ladybug

M m   mouse

N n   nail

O o   octopus

P p   puppet

Q q   queen

R r   ring

S s   socks

T t   tiger

U u   umbrella

V v   van

W w   watch

X x   X ray

Y y   yacht

Z z   zebra

Count 123

0 zero   1 one   2 two   3 three

4 four   5 five   6 six   7 seven

8 eight   9 nine   10 ten

first   second   third

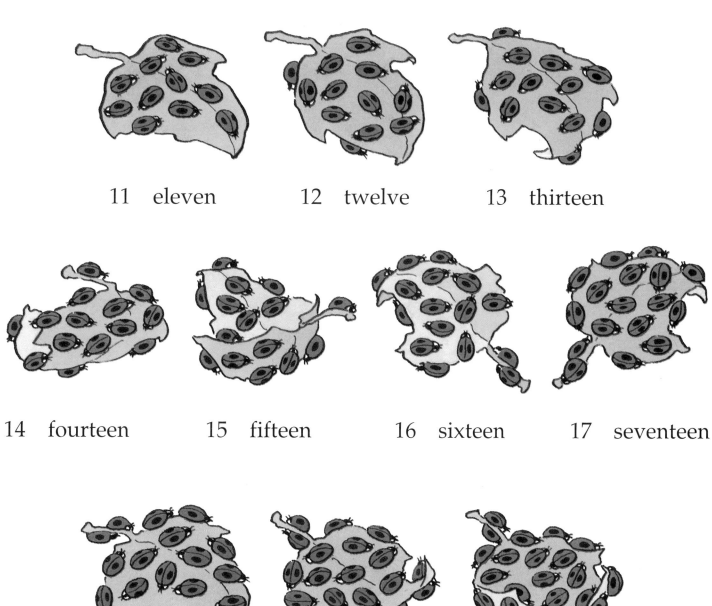

11   eleven   12   twelve   13   thirteen

14   fourteen   15   fifteen   16   sixteen   17   seventeen

18   eighteen   19   nineteen   20   twenty

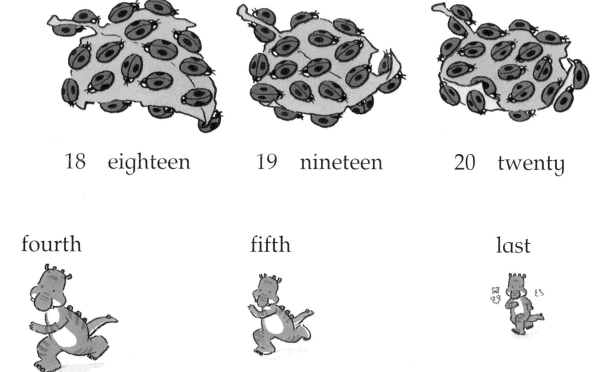

fourth   fifth   last

Shapes

rectangle

square

circle

heart

oval

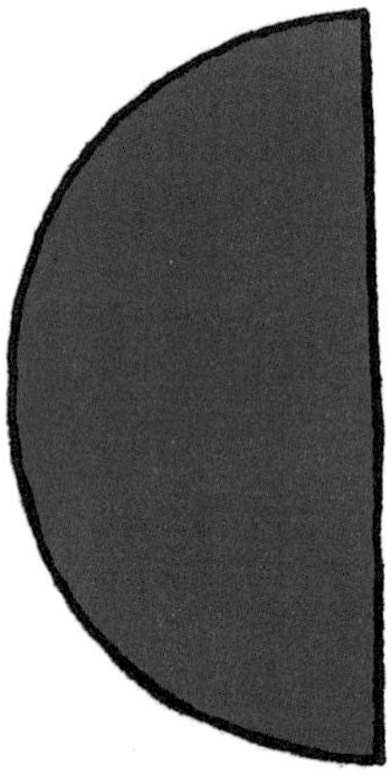

semicircle

star

triangle

pentagon

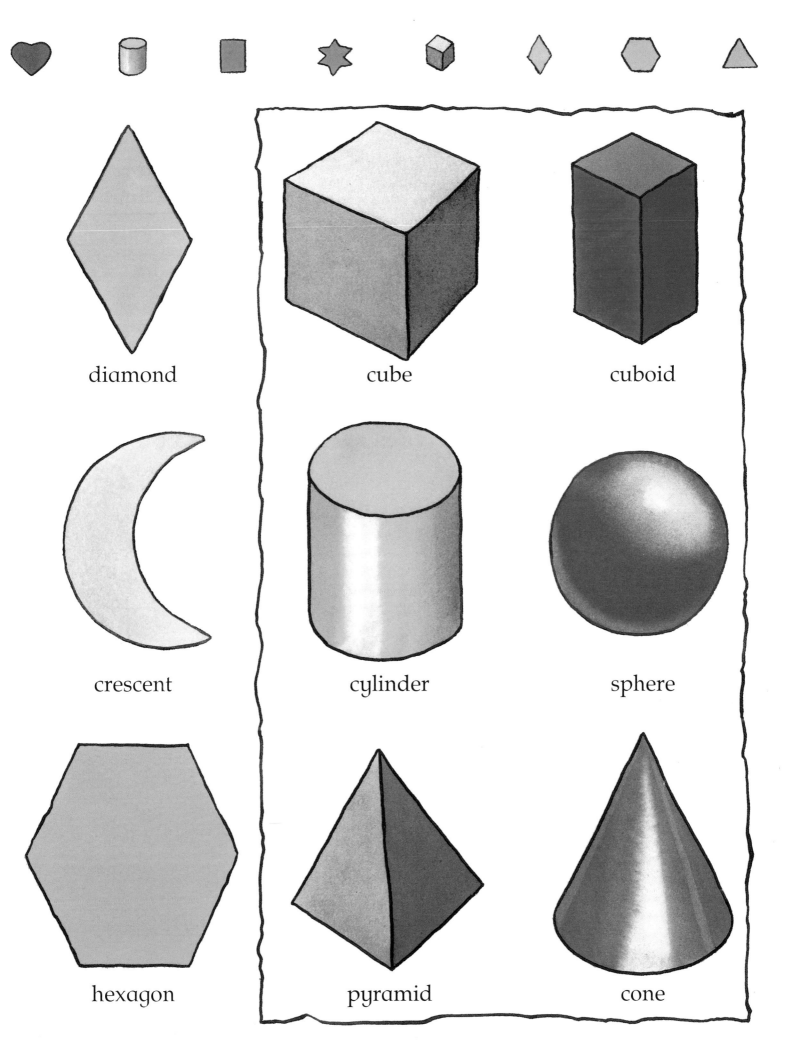

diamond

cube

cuboid

crescent

cylinder

sphere

hexagon

pyramid

cone

Opposites

big/small

clean/dirty

fat/thin

full/empty

high/low

hot/cold

new/old

open/closed

dark/light

fast/slow

happy/sad

heavy/light

long/short

more/less

same/different

wet/dry

43

cloudy

sunny

rainy

snowy

windy

foggy

8am

10am

12 noon

2pm

4pm

6pm

45

Index

46